Photographing Nature

TREES

Heather Angel MSc FIIP FRPS

First Published 1975

© Heather Angel 1975

FOUNTAIN PRESS, ARGUS BOOKS LIMITED
Station Road, Kings Langley, Hertfordshire, England

CONTENTS

INTRODUCTION

Trees are always worth photographing. No matter where they are growing, in which season, a single tree offers a multitude of subjects. I have come to appreciate and get to know trees through photography. No longer do I give trees a casual glance; instead I go towards them, feel the texture of the leaves, study the bark pattern and examine the beauty of individual catkins or flowers with a hand lens or with a long focal length lens.

Trees often feature in pictures of landscape photographers, but only rarely do nature photographers select trees or parts of trees amongst their subjects. The aim in writing this book has been to provide hints and guidelines for improving photographic techniques, as well as providing inspiration for possibly new aspects of tree photography. A practical approach has been adopted throughout, and wherever possible a photograph has been included to illustrate each technique.

So that the majority of techniques relevant to tree photography could be included in this book, it is assumed that readers will have a basic grounding in photography. All the photographic terms mentioned in this book are defined in Appendix A, and a summary of the equipment and accessories for tree photography is given in Appendix B. With the exception of Fig. 1.4, all the monochrome and most of the colour photographs were taken on a Hasselblad camera. All others were taken on a Nikkormat camera.

Each tree is a complex arrangement of bark, bole, leaves, trunk, roots and flowers – offering technically demanding, but none the less exciting subjects for both an artistic and a scientific approach. Trees are much more than static plants. Discover their qualities through the eye of a camera.

Fig. 1.1 Coconuts (*Cocos nucifera*) silhouetted against the setting sun

Trees in general

In both the temperate zones and in tropical rain forests, trees are
a dominant part of the flora. These giants of the plant kingdom
are remarkably diverse in their size, shape and form. Trees are
defined as woody plants, usually with a single stem, which are
capable of growing to at least 6 metres high. But, how different
the mental picture of a tree is in various parts of the world; in
England it is the oak, in Scandinavia the coniferous spruce, in
Canada the maple, in Australia the gum tree and on a tropical
oceanic island it is a coconut palm.

Apart from the commercial value of many trees, very often we
gain from the sheer beauty of their presence – particularly in the
case of deciduous trees in autumn. Surely no one can fail to be
motivated to expose frame after frame of golden trees rising out
of mist in a valley? Trees as a whole, and even parts of trees – at
any time of year – capture the imagination of photographers. It
is possible to enjoy trees without any expense – if not in one's
own garden, then along a roadside, in a park or in a natural woodland. Trees are not merely beautiful or useful plants; they are of
primary importance in the terrestrial ecosystem. The terrain in-
fluences the growth rate and growth pattern of a tree, and trees
in their turn affect the terrain by preventing erosion from taking
place. The air and soil temperatures, the pH (acidity or alkalinity)
of the soil, the amount of rainfall, the degree of drainage, the
amount of light and the direction of the prevailing wind, all affect
the way in which a tree grows. Persistent prevailing winds, such
as occur on high ground or on the coast, can transform a neat
symmetrical tree into a distorted – but none the less distinctive –
shape as illustrated by the hawthorn on the jacket. Biological fac-
tors also influence the growth rate of trees. These include grazing
by animals, damage by man and competition for root space and
sunlight by neighbouring trees.

Temperate trees

The trees which dominate the temperate zones are the conifers
and the deciduous broadleaved trees. Both kinds of trees bear
seeds, but in the case of conifers they are not enclosed in an
ovary. All conifers bear cones – although the juniper 'cone' is
distinctly fleshy rather than woody. The majority of conifers are

evergreens; notable exceptions being the larches, the swamp cypress and the dawn redwood. The evergreen conifers either have leaves in the form of long narrow needles, like the pines, spruces, firs and cedars, or else they have small green scale leaves like the cypresses (Plate 8). As conifers grow best in cool temperatures, they form extensive belts at high latitudes in temperate regions. They also occur at high altitudes on mountains in the tropics.

Unlike conifers, broadleaved trees (also known as hardwoods) belong to families which include shrubs and herbs as well as trees. Most of the hardwoods occur in the tropics, and those which live in temperate zones have become adapted to sub-zero winter temperatures in one of two ways. The broadleaved evergreens have developed a thick cuticle to their leaves which are retained during winter, while the deciduous hardwoods lose their leaves before the onset of winter as a precaution against water loss by evaporation when the ground is frozen. These deciduous trees outwardly show the most dramatic change from one season to another: leafing out in spring, flowering in spring or summer, changing colour in autumn and shedding leaves before winter.

Tropical trees

By contrast, trees in tropical rain forest areas are predominantly evergreen hardwoods. Other tropical trees include the palms, the cacti of American deserts and the spurge trees of African deserts. In the tropics, the year is divided into dry and wet seasons. The tropical deciduous trees tend to lose their leaves at the onset of the dry season.

Unless special precautions are taken, the high temperatures of the tropics can be detrimental to both films and cameras. If the camera is kept in an air-conditioned room, allow it to warm up to the outside temperature – inside an airtight bag – otherwise condensation will develop on both lens and film. Cameras should never be left in direct sunlight. Preferably keep them in the shade in a gadget bag, or better still, in an insulated plastic or polystyrene picnic hamper. While self-sealing polythene bags are useful for keeping individual items protected from dust or rain, they will encourage fungal growth in a humid atmosphere such as occurs in tropical rain forests.

Heat and humidity can soften the film gelatin so that when it is processed the developer penetrates the emulsion unevenly. In the damp tropical rain forest environment the air always contains microscopic fungal spores. It is therefore essential to ensure the

6

film gelatin does not contain enough moisture to permit the germination and growth of the spores. Providing the film is completely exposed within a day or two, and then stored in a tin with a drying agent, no fungal damage should result. However, if cameras are kept for several weeks in hot, humid conditions, fungi may attack the lens elements as well as the film.

Every precaution should always be taken to keep film as cool and dry as possible before, during and after exposure. The most effective drying agent is crystalline silica gel; the coloured form appears bright blue when dry and turns pale pink when it is fully saturated. Silica gel, which can be used in perforated tins or muslin bags, has the advantage of being reusable by merely drying it in an oven.

Fig. 1.2   The bizarre baobab tree (*Adansonia digitata*) – also known as the upside down tree. Kenya.

Trees in the open

So much for a brief introduction to major tree types, now to consider the various ways in which they can be photographed. A glance at the illustrations in this book will show that none include a building or a person. This is no accident. Personally, I prefer to photograph my trees for what they are as trees – preferably in their natural habitat. Whereas old photographs of trees taken by botanists and foresters nearly always included a person for a comparative scale.

Because trees change not only through the seasons but also throughout their life history, there are endless possible ways of photographing an individual specimen of a single species. The most obvious approach to tree photography is to take the tree as a whole. An isolated tree in open parkland has the advantage that it can be approached from any direction and lit from any angle. The three pictures of the English elm on page 10 show how distinct moods of a tree can be portrayed by altering the viewing position relative to the available light – in different seasons.

Lighting   In temperate regions the maximum number of hours of sunlight per day is much less during the winter than the summer months; whereas in the tropics the proportion of daylight to darkness is almost constant throughout the year. Not only are there less potential hours for photography by available light in the temperate zone winters, but also the shadows cast by the sun falling on a tree in winter will be much longer. This fact can prove an asset in monochrome photography – by emphasizing and repeating the shape of the crown as a shadow on the ground. But when working with colour filmstock, a low-angled sun casts a red glow on trees and the surrounding countryside. While this time of day can be used to advantage for landscape pictures of silhouetted trees against a setting sun (see Plate 24), it is not ideal for recording the true colours of trunk and leaves.

At mid-day, when the sun is at its highest point in the sky, the air molecules selectively scatter more blue and less green or red wavelengths so that the sun appears yellow and the sky blue. Whereas when the sun is low in the sky, the light strikes the earth at an oblique angle, thereby passing through a greater distance of the earth's atmosphere. Much more scattering takes place, so that fewer of the shorter blue and green wavelengths pass through and therefore the long red wavelengths predominate, and are seen on earth as a red cast.

Even though more wavelengths of all colours reach the earth at mid-day, this is not an ideal time for photographing trees – or for taking any landscape pictures. For at this time there are no subtle combinations of light and shadow which help to model the subject and to provide some apparent depth in a two-dimensional picture. If the direction or the strength of the sunlight is not ideal for the particular subject, then make a mental note of what time of day you should return – either later on the same day – or sometime the following day.

The light intensity can be measured on either a separate photoelectric meter or a through-the-lens (TTL) meter built into the camera. When the meter is pointed towards the subject (as with TTL meters), it measures the light *reflected* from it. A more accurate method of measuring a small pale subject against a dark background (or vice versa) is to point the meter, fitted with a diffusing cone, in the subject-to-camera direction, so that the light falling on the subject (*incident* light) is measured. Incorrect measurement of light intensity is usually the basis of incorrect exposures. The exposure latitude on colour films is small, so that exposure by guesswork is both a waste of time and film.

For bold silhouettes on monochrome or colour film, the direction of the light source must be behind the subject. Care should be taken to ensure that direct rays from the sun do not enter the lens – although the likelihood of flare is now greatly reduced by modern multi-coated lenses. In any case, it is always a wise precaution to use a lens hood and to move into a position where the trunk or a branch shields the majority of direct sun rays from the lens. For the most effective emphasis of outline branch shapes, expose as if the tree was in sunlight – in other words underexpose for the tree in shadow. Monochrome is a particularly suitable medium for silhouettes. For maximum extremes of white background and black subject, under-expose and over-develop the film and print on contrasty paper. Examples of monochrome silhouettes can be seen on pages 4, 10 and 24.

Some people argue that a silhouette does not constitute a nature photograph. To my mind however, providing the camera lens does not distort the perspective unduly, then a silhouette is a justifiable means of emphasizing shape at the expense of texture. Both the pollarded beech (Fig. 2.3) and the bois rouge leaves (Fig. 3.3) convey their biological story better with a simplified bold two-dimensional image.

While open grown parkland trees show the most typical growth form and are readily accessible, they very often cannot

Fig. 1.3
English elm tree (*Ulmus procera*)
TL In winter. Diffuse lighting on overcast day.

BR In summer.
Against the light in full sunlight

BL In summer. Direct side lighting.

provide the atmosphere comparable with a less perfect tree in a woodland or on a hillside. Also, there is always the tendency to position a single tree in the centre of the frame, which can only result in a series of mere record shots. Note how I have varied the position of the elm tree in each picture on page 10. Parks and arboreta are none the less good places to get to know trees, because many specimens will be labelled. Then, when the growth form of individual species becomes familiar, they can be singled out from amongst other trees in a forest.

In Britain, it is advisable to get permission from the relevant authority of a public place or a park, for the erection of a tripod – which may not be allowed on safety grounds. If in doubt, it will be wiser to hand-hold the camera.

Choice of lens   As always, the choice of which lens to use for a particular subject is all important. If you want to photograph the entire length of a tall tree growing in a confined space then a wide angle lens will have to be used and the camera tilted. While this will enable the entire tree to be photographed, it will produce a distorted picture of the tree. This is less obvious when photographing a single tree than a group of trees, which will appear to have their crowns leaning in towards the centre of the frame. This distortion is increased with the viewing angle of the lens and so is more obvious with a wide angle than a standard lens. There are instances when intentional perspective distortion can be used to advantage, as shown in Fig. 2.4.

Therefore if an entire tree is to be photographed with the least possible distortion, it is better to stand further away and use a standard or even a long lens – without tilting the camera – than to move in close with a wide angle lens. For an artist who uses a photograph as a basis for an accurate reference drawing of a tree, then a distortion-free photograph is essential. For this purpose, as well as for architectural work, a special kind of wide angle lens, known as a perspective correcting (PC) lens, is ideal. This type of lens, which is made by several manufacturers, corrects the perspective distortion due to tilting the camera, by off-centring the lens. Figure 1.4 compares a group of pine trees photographed with a conventional 35mm wide angle lens and with a 35mm PC Nikkor lens.

Isolation from background   Individual trees or groups of trees can be isolated from their surroundings in one of several ways. An effective, but not always predictable method, is the combination

11

of sun and shadow or light and shade: a shaft of sunlight may momentarily light up a tree in its full autumn glory against a dark stormy sky. Alternatively, a tree can be emphasized by silhouetting it against the late evening sky as shown by the mangrove in Plate 24.

Another method which can be useful for isolating trees – especially from an unsightly background – is more applicable to mountain and moorland regions in temperate climates than the tropics. The days when the mist swirls through a valley are ideal for blotting out factories or pit heaps. The rowan tree in Fig. 1.5 was photographed on one such day in Snowdonia in December.

On a bright sunny day, filters placed over the camera lens can be used to define trees more clearly amongst their surroundings. For monochrome films, strongly coloured contrast filters can be useful, but will necessitate an exposure increase, which can easily be adjusted with TTL metering. A yellow filter darkens blue sky and therefore makes clouds more obvious. A red filter will also darken the sky as well as green foliage and ground shadows.

Providing the camera is used at right angles to the sun, the sky can also be darkened on both monochrome and colour film by using a polarizing filter. This is the only filter which will darken a blue sky without upsetting the colour balance of the film and therefore the colours in the rest of the scene. For more distant shots of trees – especially when working near the coast or at altitude – an ultra-violet absorbing filter, known as a haze filter, is always useful for eliminating haze.

Recording　Even though trees are more permanent than animals, it may well save a return journey if adequate field notes are made at the same time as the photographic session. Notes, which should include leaf shape, bark texture and colour as well as overall shape of the tree and the habitat, can be written into a hard-backed field notebook or dictated into an electronic pocket tape recorder. The latter saves time on the spot, but the information will still have to be written down at a later date. If an interesting tree is discovered by chance, it will be worth noting the grid reference from a large scale map, so that the tree can be found again.

Recording the names of trees which are labelled in parks and arboreta can save hours of work pouring over reference books – but it is still a wise precaution to check the identification as soon as possible – since labels have been known to be wrong.

Fig. 1.4 Scots pine (*Pinus sylvestris*) woodland in spring.
T   Taken with a 35mm wide angle lens.
B   Taken with a 35mm perspective correcting lens.

Fig. 1.5 Rowan tree (*Sorbus aucuparia*) in winter, isolated by valley mist in Snowdonia.

Trees in season

Evergreen trees, and most especially the formal solid forms such as the columnar funeral cypress, which is such a feature of Mediterranean landscapes, and the clipped Irish yews so typical of old English churchyards, offer the least possible scope for variation in photography during different months of the year. When photographing into the light, these trees become dark solid forms with perhaps some relief from rim lighting. Whereas pines, spruces and firs allow light to pass through their more open branches from the front, the side or behind. Apart from the direction of the light source, some variation in photographs of conifers can be gained during different seasons: in winter the green branches may be laiden with snow; in spring they become flushed with yellow as the male catkins release their microscopic pollen grains.

Deciduous conifers such as larch, swamp cypress and dawn redwood, turn a wonderful range of hues in autumn. The basis behind this colour change is described in Chapter 5. Deciduous trees in general offer a much greater range in gradation of colour and tone throughout the year. Bare winter skeletons of deciduous trees are best photographed in the gentle diffuse sunlight of slightly overcast days, when the tips of the fine branches are resolved most clearly (Fig. 1.3 TL). Still greater emphasis – with additional colour – can be gained by waiting until the buds begin to break in spring, flushing the whole tree a gentle pale green.

Forest trees

When trees grow up in close confinement with other trees in woodlands or forests, their characteristic symmetrical open growth form becomes greatly modified. No longer do they develop a deep rounded crown, with branches maybe extending down to ground level; instead the side branches die back in the upward struggle for light. This 'race for light', is more apparent in an evergreen tropical rain forest than in a deciduous temperate woodland. When an old tree falls in a tropical rain forest, it opens up the overhead canopy, thereby allowing a shaft of sunlight to spotlight the forest floor, where a dense growth of saplings soon develops.

Woods and forests are not merely collections of trees; they are distinct habitats in which a variety of plants and animals constantly interact. Deciduous woodlands undergo the most dramatic change with season. As the leaves begin to open in spring,

15

a beech wood becomes flushed with a delicate green. In summer, when the leaves have fully opened and turned a dark green, the wood seems more sombre; but by autumn it becomes a riot of yellows and golds (Plate 1). Only in winter can the form and shape of the solid greyish trunks be fully appreciated.

Old woods in which only a few large trees remain standing are much easier for photography than the tightly packed, evenly spaced formation which is so typical of young coniferous forests. Even though more light will reach the forest floor in old woods where trees have fallen, photography on bright sunny days is not easy in any forest. Then, the extremes of light and shade may be so great that they cannot be satisfactorily recorded on colour film. On the other hand, when the sun filters through a light cloud cover, the level of light intensity is reduced into a more uniform diffuse lighting. Under these conditions, when little or no wind is blowing, better colour photographs can be taken by using a tripod. In fact, a tripod is invaluable when working in woodlands – for photographing not only trees, but also fungi, mosses and lichens.

While gentle diffuse lighting produces pleasanter colour pictures; direct side lighting can produce dramatic effects when photographing a stand of regular boles on monochrome; as shown in Fig. 1.6. Indeed, this approach is often the only way to illustrate a dense coniferous forest – apart from a distorted view from inside looking straight up through the crowns. As already explained, a standard or a long focus lens will produce less distortion of woodland trees than a wide angle lens – unless it is a perspective correcting lens.

Coniferous forests are typified by having few herbaceous plants at ground level. Whereas both deciduous forests (especially in the spring) and tropical rain forests have a conspicuous understorey of plants and shrubs. If this understorey obscures the field of view of the trees themselves, it may be necessary to climb up above it – either by using a step-ladder or by climbing a tree. At ground level, tropical rain forest appears a bewildering jungle of trunks, saplings, lianas and leaves, but above the sapling layer the full splendour of the massive trunks – often supported by buttress roots – becomes apparent. It takes some ingenuity to use a tripod effectively whilst perched precariously on a ladder or up a tree; but it can be done by supporting the legs at right angles to the trunk. A tree clamp, with a ball-and-socket head, is a more practical camera support if clamped onto the top of a step-ladder than onto a bough of a tree – which is never in the right place.

Fig. 1.6 A side-lit stand of larch (*Larix decidua*) boles, taken with a long focus lens.

As has been mentioned on page 6, the hot, humid conditions of tropical rain forests, can create serious problems for the photographer. Apart from the biting insects, other features of these forests include heavy fruit which periodically come crashing down and drip tips on the ends of simple leaves. Rain drains off these leaves onto any objects – including cameras – below. An umbrella is therefore useful for protecting equipment from a steady stream of these drips, which may continue for up to two hours after a rain shower has stopped.

Infra-red photography

Plant ecologists use aerial photography as a tool for calculating the proportion of different tree species in impenetrable forests. Monochrome pictures of mixed forests will show up the difference between evergreen and deciduous trees only in winter, in early spring and in autumn. Throughout the growing season, when both are in full leaf, they cannot always be distinguished with certainty. But because evergreens and deciduous trees absorb and reflect different amounts of infra-red wavelengths, it is possible to distinguish between them on infra-red film. Deciduous trees which reflect more infra-red light than evergreens, appear white on infra-red prints, whereas evergreens appear dark. Colour infra-red film reproduces false, but dramatic colours: deciduous trees appear as a magenta colour, while evergreens are bluish.

As several infra-red films are available in 35mm cassettes, any 35mm camera can be used – but a modern lens which has an infra-red mark on the lens mounting, will ensure more accurate focusing of the long invisible infra-red wavelengths at the maximum lens aperture. A small lens aperture, such as $f/11$, will ensure maximum definition by increasing the depth of field and thereby compensating for the discrepancy between the visible plane of focus and the actual infra-red plane of focus.

As infra-red films are also sensitive to visible wavelengths, either a red filter such as a Wratten 25 should be used to absorb blue and green light, or a Wratten 87, 88A or 89B to absorb all visible light. The ratio of infra-red radiation to visible radiation is not constant and so infra-red films cannot be given an exact speed rating.

The use of infra-red film is by no means confined to scientific applications: it can also be used for penetrating haze and for unusual pictorial effects of landscape photographs with trees.

Fig. 1.7 Himalayan pines (*Pinus wallichiana*) taken with a long focus lens from horseback in Kashmir.

Fig. 2.1   Old olive (*Olea europaea*) trunks. Corfu.

CHAPTER 2   BOLE AND BARK

After photographing a tree as a whole, it is well worth moving in closer to concentrate attention on the trunk alone. The un-branched part of the trunk is referred to as the bole.

Trunks

The trunk supports the branches of a tree and also contains an elaborate internal transport system. Water and nutrients are carried up from the roots to the leaves; while food manufactured in the leaves is carried down to feed the rest of the tree. The shape, size and colour of trunks show considerable variation. Examples are the absurdly obese trunk of the African baobab tree (Fig. 1.2) the spiny giant cactus trunk (Plate 4) and the gnarled, twisted trunks of old olives (Fig. 2.1).

While trunks of young saplings will bend in the wind, trunks in general are the most rigid part of the tree, and can therefore be photographed on a windy day by using a long exposure. For the least distorted view of a trunk, photograph it with a standard or a long focus lens – preferably working at a good camera to subject distance with the camera parallel to the ground. On uneven ground, the level of the camera can be checked with a spirit level.

Using a vertical format, the frame can be filled with a single broad trunk. If the trunk is too slender or the working distance too large for the trunk to fill the frame, try varying its position in the frame by off-centring it. Pictorial interest may be gained by including out-of-focus leaves in the foreground or by shadow patterns cast by the leaves.

The photography of the trunks of evergreen trees can be difficult because of the problem of the deep shadows cast by the lowest branches. Open grown trees will tend to be much bushier in their growth form with dense low branches, whereas woodland trees grow straighter and shed their lower branches. For photographing trunk patterns, look for examples of woodland trees which have become isolated by the felling of neighbouring trees.

Winter is a good season for photographing the trunks of deciduous trees. More light penetrates down through the bare branches and because the sun is lower in the sky, it casts more conspicuous shadows on uneven textured trunks. If the ground is snow-covered, additional light will be reflected up onto the base of the bole. Trunks which have a spiny or thorny coating are especially suitable subjects for photographing against the light. Plate 4 shows how effective this rim lighting is for a spiny cactus.

Not only are naturally shaped trunks worth photographing, but so are the irregular deformed trunks which result from coppicing or pollarding. Coppicing is the repeated cutting of a broadleaved tree at ground level to produce fencing poles. Extensive areas of coppiced hazel and sweet chestnut woodlands still exist in Europe. A recently coppiced woodland lets in plenty of light and so encourages the growth of carpets of spring flowers, such as primroses or bluebells. The practice of repeated cutting across a tree about two metres from the ground – called pollarding – encourages the growth of numerous small trunks well beyond the reach of browsing animals. Apart from willows and planes growing in built-up areas, trees are no longer pollarded today; however, several hundred-year-old beech and oak pollards still stand. Figure 2.3 shows an intact pollarded beech in the New Forest, England.

Bark

Bark is the outer protective layer of a tree. It is often so distinctive, that it alone can be used as a sole means of identification. Bark ranges from the thin constantly peeling skin of the eucalyptus trees to the fibrous 30cm thick coat of redwoods. The form of bark can vary even on a single tree – the trunk bark often being quite distinct from the branch bark. Older bark consists of several layers, including an outer cork layer. This layer is exceptionally thick in the cork oak and is removed from the tree about every ten years. If the bark continues to grow as the tree increases in girth, then it either remains smooth as in beech or it peels off in thin strips (birches) or in flakes (plane). Whereas a rough, irregular bark is caused by the outer cork layer dying and the bark becoming cracked by the pressure from the growth of the sapwood within.

Like the trunk, bark pictures are particularly suitable subjects to work on during the winter months, when trees – especially deciduous trees – are in their least interesting phase: no leaves, no flowers and only some persistent fruit remain over winter. When the bark has a large bold pattern, both the shape of the trunk and the design of the bark can be combined in a single picture. The bark of many trees forms a repetitive pattern, which is best emphasized by filling the entire frame (Fig. 2.5).

Fig. 2.2 Young beech (*Fagus sylvatica*) trunks outlined by snow.

Fig. 2.3   Silhouetted pollarded beech tree (*Fagus sylvatica*). New Forest, Hampshire

Strong cross or grazed lighting from a low angled sun early or late in the day will accentuate bark texture – especially the vertical fissures of sweet chestnut (Fig. 2.5 BL) and coastal redwood. The transverse intermittent markings on the bark of cherries and some birches usually contrast well against the overall colour or tone of the trunk, so that critical lighting is not so essential (Fig. 2.5 TL). Some palms on the other hand, have circular leaf base scars. These tend to merge in with the trunk unless lit from overhead so that they are accentuated by their shadows.

Resin The distinctive smell of pine and fir woods is caused by resins secreted by the trees. Commercial quantities of crude turpentine are obtained from some of these trees – including the Aleppo pine – by cutting the bark and collecting the resinous secretions. These resins, which are a by-product of life processes, are beneficial in wound healing and as fungicides. The Australian gum trees also produce resins. In some areas, yellow lumps of fossilized resin or amber can be dug from the ground in which resinous trees – such as the New Zealand kauri pine – flourished. These gum fossils – especially if they contain a trapped insect – offer wonderful scope for photography by means of transmitted light. But even the fresh white resinous secretions can provide additional contrast to a bark pattern or a cone.

Hangers-on

While climbing, epiphytic and parasitic plants which grow on trees are botanically quite distinct from them, they are none the less so closely associated with the trunk that it seems logical to include them in this chapter.

Climbers Plants which grow up from ground level and use the trunk as a means of support to gain height in their growth towards the light, are known as climbers. The majority do no physical damage to the tree if it is well established, but woody climbers such as honeysuckle, can distort the stems of young saplings. Scrambling plants use curved hooks, gourds use tendrils, while ivy uses roots to gain a foothold on trunks. Virginia creeper (Plate 22) has evolved an elaborate means of ensuring it has no chance of being blown down: branch tips swell into little cushions which cling to a tree or a wall by producing a sticky substance.

Climbing plants can add both interest and colour to a trunk

25

Plate 1   New Forest Ancient and Ornamental woodland
showing beeches (*Fagus sylvatica*) in autumn.
Wide angle lens (opposite).

Plate 2   Bole of hardwood tree infected with parasitic
sulphur polypore fungus (*Grifola sulphurea*).
Diffuse natural lighting.

which is not particularly photogenic in itself. The very fact that these plants are climbers means that they will often be growing in forests which are poorly lit at ground level. Climbers which have a compact growth form will hardly move in the wind and so can be photographed on a slow film using a long exposure with the camera steadied on a tripod or a tree clamp. Whereas climbers with larger leaves or leaves with long leaf stalks, will quiver even in the slightest breeze and will therefore appear as a blurred image with a long exposure. The solution is then either to use a fast film and a fast shutter speed or to use flashlight. Unlike several branches of animal photography a flash is by no means essential for photographing trees; but it can be extremely useful for arresting movement, for increasing depth of field in close-ups and for isolating part of a tree from its surroundings. As the intensity of flashlight (or any other point source) falls off by the square of the distance, a flash will only satisfactorily light parts of trees in close-up both in the field and indoors. It is totally unsuitable for general woodland pictures.

In the long run, a small electronic flash will work out to be more economical than buying hundreds of flash bulbs. The type of shutter in the camera will determine the fastest shutter speed which can be used with electronic flash. Most 35mm SLR cameras have a focal plane shutter, which synchronizes only when the complete frame is exposed at one time – usually at 1/30 or 1/60 second, but on some models at 1/125 second. A camera which has a diaphragm or leaf shutter can be synchronized at any speed with electronic flash.

Epiphytes   Unlike climbers, epiphytes have no connection with the soil at ground level. Although they grow on the tree itself, they gain no nourishment from it. Larger epiphytic plants such as ferns, bromeliads and orchids, tend to grow in a branch fork where humus collects. Microscopic algae, small lichens and mosses on the other hand, grow directly on the vertical trunks, on the branches and even on small twigs.

Epiphytes are small plants which have solved the problem of getting adequate sunlight in forests, as a result they are better lit but often completely inaccessible. They tend to be more abundant on rough-barked than on smooth-barked trees. Epiphytes flourish in damper rather than drier environments. Finely branching epiphytes like beard lichens and Spanish moss (not a true moss, but a bromeliad), hang down as delicate curtains, relieving the sombre shape of dark trunks. Although Spanish moss will

Fig. 2.4   Intentional perspective distortion of *Eucalyptus* trunks with a wide angle lens. Kenya.

Plate 3 Old stag-headed oak tree (*Quercus robur*) leafing out in spring. Wide angle lens.

Plate 4   Natural back lighting emphasizes the spiny coating of the *Opuntia* cactus in the Galapagos.

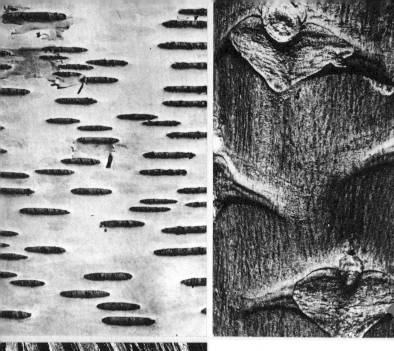

Fig. 2.5
Bark patterns

TL   A North American birch
      (*Betula sandbergi*).

BL   Sweet chestnut
      (*Castanea sativa*).

TR   Leaf scars of papaw
      (*Carica papaya*).

drape itself over any support – including telegraph wires – it is most photogenic festooning the branches of American live oaks.

Most epiphytes, and particularly small encrusting lichens, are subjects for close-up photography. The cheapest way to get in close is to use a close-up or a supplementary lens on the front of the camera lens. However, a close-up lens, no matter how good, will reduce the resolving power of the lens itself. The one major advantage of a close-up lens is that it absorbs no light, so that no exposure increase is required, and it may well be preferable to extension tubes when photographing a moving subject on a dull day with a slow colour film. Cameras which have an inter-changeable lens system, can have extension tubes or bellows in-serted between the camera body and the lens for close-up photography. They both reduce the amount of light reaching the film, so that the exposure must be increased. With TTL metering the exposure can be adjusted very quickly, but with all other cameras it will have to be calculated from the data supplied with the extension tubes or bellows. Leafy lichens growing flush with the trunk can be photographed only with the camera at right angles to the trunk. Diffuse lighting is often most suitable when photographing pastel-coloured lichens on colour film; whereas side or grazed lighting will bring up the surface texture on monochrome. Beard lichens and ferns which grow out from the bark are effective if lit from behind.

Parasites Parasites, like epiphytes, are smaller than the plant on which they grow. But unlike them they feed on their host tree. Some flowering plants (including mistletoe) and many fungi are parasitic on trees. Several larger bracket fungi (Plate 2) cause serious heart rot to trees which then become weakened and more liable to being blown down in a gale.

The techniques for photographing tree parasites are similar to those described for epiphytes; and if the parasite is known to be confined to a single tree species, it is worth trying to include some distinctive feature such as part of the bark or some leaves. Photographs of climbers, epiphytes and parasites can be used to illustrate yet another facet about the biology of a particular species of tree.

Plate 5   London plane (*Platanus* × *hispanica*) bole with characteristic flaking bark. Medium long focus lens.

Plate 6   Open grown Atlas cedar (*Cedrus atlantica*) in spring. Medium long focus lens.

Fig. 3.1   Screwpine or vacoa leaves
(Pandanus hornei). Seychelles.

Leaves are the most important part of a tree. It is here that photo-synthesis – the process whereby sugars are manufactured from carbon dioxide and water in the presence of sunlight – takes place. The food is then transported from the leaves, which may number as many as 250,000 in a large oak, to the rest of the tree. Leaves from a single species of tree conform to the same basic design but no two leaves are absolutely identical. The life of a leaf is relatively short – about six months on average. Even ever-green leaves are shed and replaced.

Leaf design

The leaf shape is related both to the climatic conditions of the country of origin and to the arrangement of the leaves on the twig or branch. Evergreen conifers reduce their water loss during the winter months by either having tiny scale leaves or needles with a thick cuticle and enrolled margins. These types of leaves offer little scope for imaginative approaches to lighting. Large needles can be silhouetted with cones *in situ* on a branch; but small scales can be shown only by close-up photographs taken under controlled conditions indoors. Carpets of needles on a forest floor may provide interesting close-up shots.

The leaves of evergreen hardwoods also have a thick cuticle, but they are usually larger and flatter than conifers. Olive, orange and rhododendrons are evergreens with simple leaves. Many deciduous trees, including alder, beech, lime, poplar and willow, also have simple leaves. Leaves which are divided into several leaflets such as in ash, walnut and hickory, are called compound leaves. If the leaflets arise from the same place on the leaf stalk they form a palmate leaf, as in the horse chestnut.

Leaves in situ

Leaf mosaics   In temperate regions leaves of broadleaved trees grow orientated to the light so that their upper surfaces receive the maximum amount of sunlight. Each species has a character-istic arrangement of the leaves on a twig, which may be in a spiral, an alternate or an opposite pattern. These leaf patterns, which are known as leaf mosaics, make excellent photographic subjects.

It is the larger leaves which produce the most photogenic leaf mosaic patterns. Select small branches isolated from the rest of

Plate 7 Sunlight streaming through black gum (*Nyssa sylvatica*) leaves in autumn.

Plate 8   Pink male and blue female cones of Lawson cypress
(*Chamaecyparis lawsoniana*). Studio with flash. ×2

Fig. 3.2 Long focus lens used to isolate a single olive (*Olea europaea*) branch against sea and islands. Corfu.

the tree – particularly the main overhead canopy – and focus on a few leaves with a long focus lens. Freshly opened leaves are less likely to be damaged by wind or insects, and are often a more interesting colour than older, mature leaves. Deciduous temperate trees such as beech, leaf out in a delicate pale green colour which lasts for a few brief weeks before the leaves thicken and darken with age.

Viewed against the light, evergreen and mature deciduous leaves will be silhouetted. In contrast, young or thin leaves will be transilluminated by the sunlight filtering through them (Plate 7). Where the leaf edges overlap, the tones are darkened in monochrome and intensified in colour. Transillumination clearly shows up the venation pattern. Figure 3.3 shows both the outline shape and the arrangement of the bois rouge leaves. The numerous holes (caused by weevils) are such a distinctive feature, that they can be used to recognize the tree in the field. The holes also relieve what would otherwise be a very heavy silhouette.

Small leaves, and leaves on low trees hemmed in by other trees, cannot easily be isolated against the sky. They can, however, be isolated in other ways. A branch may be highlighted by sun against a background in deep shadow, or flashlight can be used to create a similar effect. Strong side lighting is effective for long leaves growing out at different angles from the trunk like the screwpine leaves in Fig. 3.1.

Shiny leaves   Direct sunlight or flashlight falling on glossy leaves can produce distracting reflections, so an overcast day when the sunlight is diffuse is better for photographing such leaves. A diffusing screen, such as sheets of muslin held between the sun and the leaves; or flashlight bounced off a white board or a white umbrella, will give a similar effect. For real close-up shots of leaves or parts of a leaf, adjusting either the camera position relative to the sun or the position of the flash relative to the camera, may be sufficient to ease the problem. This is an instance when a SLR camera is essential for seeing precisely when and where the reflections appear in the field of view. A flashlight with a built-in modelling lamp will be a great asset here; but a small torch light strapped to the flash, is a cheap alternative.

Distracting highlights can also be reduced by attaching a polarizing filter to the front of the camera lens. The best camera angle for the particular subject, will be found by moving a SLR camera and slowly rotating the polarizing filter in its mount until the reflections are least conspicuous. TTL metering is ideal

Plate 9   Norway spruce (*Picea abies*) cones lying amongst moss on forest floor.

Plate 10   Massed winged fruits of smooth-leaved elm (*Ulmus carpinifolia*).

Fig. 3.3 Bois rouge (*Dillenia ferruginea*) leaf mosaic. Seychelles.

for achieving the correct exposure with complete or partial polarization.

Leaf portraits

The photographer who enjoys close-up photography has plenty of scope amongst parts of trees. Buds, leaves, catkins, flowers, fruit, cones and galls are all suitable for close-up work – especially indoors. Inside a studio the direction and strength of the light source(s) and the colour of the background can be selected to emphasize the shape or the colour of the subject in detailed close-up portraits. A macro lens, capable of focusing down to half life size, is ideal for studio close-ups.

Collection Pieces should not be removed from a tree without the consent of the owner, nor if they will cause any injury to the tree. Often the choicest spray is impossible to reach from ground level without the help of a pair of long-armed pruners or a step-ladder. On a recently felled tree, however, even the uppermost branches will be accessible. Before a branch is removed from a standing tree, carefully note its growth angle – and more especially the positioning of the leaves – so that they can be orientated and illuminated as naturally as possible in the studio. This is especially important for foliage which naturally hangs down.

Props All advantages gained by bringing the subject indoors will be lost if either the subject itself, or the camera, are not firmly supported. Sloppy techniques may be excusable when working under harsh conditions in the field, but they are inexcusable indoors. Either a standard tripod resting on the floor, or a small table-top tripod placed directly on the bench or table, should be used to support the camera. For supporting a branch in an upright position, use either plasticine, a jar of wet sand or a florist's heavy spiky base. A pendulous branch can be held in position by means of a clamp stand or a clothes peg on a line.

The choice of background is also important for close-up portraits. The most natural is additional foliage out-of-focus behind the subject. The most dramatic (for both monochrome and colour) is black velvet – providing it is kept free of creases and cloth fragments. Other suitable backgrounds include uniformly blue-coloured artists' boards to simulate sky or mottled greens and browns to simulate natural out-of-focus settings of foliage and earth. Textured backgrounds such as woven cloths are seldom suitable – unless they are moved during the exposure to produce

Plate 11   Shiny fruit of raffia palm (*Raphia ruffia*) taken in direct sunlight, Seychelles. ×2

Plate 12   Female flower or 'rose' of European larch (*Larix decidua*) with yellow pollen grains. Studio, dual source oblique lighting. ×7

a blurred effect. As a general rule, choose dark backgrounds for light-coloured leaves and keep light ones for dark leaves. For monochrome work, grey makes a good background tone for most subjects. When the subject completely fills the frame, there is, of course, no need for a separate background.

Lighting   Natural sunlight streaming in through a window or a conservatory, can be used as the sole light source indoors. However, as studio work is usually done during bad weather or at night, an artificial light source such as flashlight or photofloods, is most often used. Artificial lighting has the advantages of being constant and being more easily controlled.

The direction of the light source(s) should be carefully selected for each individual subject and its background. For instance, if frontal lighting is used with a pale background, unsightly shadows from the subject may be cast onto the background behind. This is why a black background is such an asset because it absorbs all shadows.

Although completely frontal lighting, such as a ring flash, may ease the shadow problem, it lacks any modelling. Most leaves can therefore be better lit by using single or dual source oblique lighting. If the lights are angled in towards the subject from in front, and the background is placed several centimetres away from the subject, the shadows will fall outside the field of view of close-ups. With a single light source, it may be necessary to fill in the shadow it casts on one side of the subject, by using a white card to throw back some of the light. Using a continuous light source such as photofloods – or better still, narrow beamed spotlights – the precise effect of light and shadow can be critically viewed through a SLR camera and, if necessary, modified. With photofloods or spotlights, an overall false colour cast will be apparent unless artificial light colour film is used, or daylight colour film with a colour conversion filter such as a Wratten 80B.

Extreme side lighting, with the light source on a level with the subject, is known as grazed or textured lighting. This is particularly suitable for showing up the surface texture – especially the veins of leaves – in monochrome. The leaf can be laid on a flat surface, or if it is stuck down onto board with small pieces of 'Blu-tak' on its underside, it can be propped up at right angles to the bench top.

Back lighting – already mentioned for photography in the field in previous chapters – is more likely to be successful in the studio because lens flare can be controlled. One or two light

Fig. 3.4 Part of monkey puzzle (*Araucaria araucana*) stem showing spiral arrangement of flattened leaves.

Plate 13   *Magnolia* × *soulangeana* fruit supported on sheet of glass and lit with two oblique light sources from above.

Plate 14   Detail of horse chestnut (*Aesculus hippocastanum*) flowers. Dual source oblique lighting in studio. × 4

sources are directed onto the subject from behind. Hairy or spiny leaf margins are rim lit and stand out against the dark background and thick veins are differentiated from the leaf as a whole. The direction of the light source can be more critically controlled by using a narrow beamed spotlight or by extending the outer margin of a light or a flash with a tube of matt black paper.

Skeleton leaves which have had all but their veins eaten or rotted away, provide endless scope for different lighting techniques. They can be back lit against a black background, they can be lit by transmitted light and they can be used for making photograms (page 57). Transmitted light is also ideal for photographing translucent leaves. A cheap version of the light box sold for viewing transparencies, can be made by painting an old drawer white. One or more strip lights are fixed inside the bottom and the top covered with a sheet of opal glass which acts as a diffuser. The leaf is placed directly on the opal glass, and if necessary flattened with a piece of clear glass. Care must be taken not to allow living leaves to become too warm – otherwise they will wilt. The camera is mounted vertically overhead. A skeleton leaf will be reproduced as a silhouette of veins against a pale background, while a living leaf will be delicately transilluminated.

Dark field illumination is a special kind of transmitted lighting, by which the subject appears brightly lit against a black background. The leaf is placed on a glass plate about 15cm above a matt black background. A ring of small torch or Christmas tree lights (powered by a battery or the mains) are placed beneath the glass plate and angled in towards the subject, but outside the field of view of the overhead camera. Care must be taken to ensure no light falls directly on the camera lens, but only light which is refracted or scattered by the subject. When dark field illumination is combined with careful top lighting, the surface detail as well as fine hairy margins of a leaf can be illustrated in a single picture.

The problem of distracting highlights on shiny leaves – which is often accentuated by using multiple light sources in a studio – can be solved by one of the various ways outlined on page 41. Diffuse rather than direct light sources will certainly help. If all else fails, spray the leaf with the Aerosol matt spray used by film cameramen to dull shiny surfaces.

Time lapse photography To portray the very subtle movements involved in the opening of a bud or a flower, a series of pictures will have to be taken at known intervals. Unlike high-speed photography, this time lapse photography can be done with a basic camera with no additional equipment. Due to the variation in natural lighting, a great deal of patience is required for getting a good field sequence. Indoors, the lighting can be controlled by using photofloods or flashlight at a fixed distance from the subject.

Throughout the sequence, the camera to subject distance and angle must be kept constant; otherwise comparative measurements cannot be taken from individual frames. Therefore the camera must be rigidly supported. Resist the impulse to fill the frame with a tight bud – otherwise either the leaves will open outside the field of view or else the magnification will have to be decreased. Play safe by positioning the bud in the first frame slightly below the centre, and thereby allowing space for the leaves to open out at any angle. Still time lapse photographs are usually made on separate frames; but multiple exposures can be made on a single frame by recocking the shutter without winding on the film (Fig. 3.5). The time interval between successive exposures, will vary for different subjects – it may be as long as several hours or even days. There is always a greater risk of moving the camera when changing a film, so try to expose a complete series on a single film. In the long run, both time and film can be saved by spending a day or two taking no pictures and recording the total time it takes for a bud or flower to open fully. Then by dividing this time by the total number of exposures per film, the time interval between each exposure can be calculated.

The interval between exposures can either be timed manually, or automatically with a timing unit such as a mechanical clock or an electric timer. If an automatic timer is used with a motorized camera, the set-up can be left to run unattended. An extra long length of film in a special camera body or magazine will be needed for a long run of time exposures. Several motorized camera bodies are available which enable 250 consecutive exposures to be made on 35mm film and one which allows over 500 exposures on 6×6cm film.

Leaf prints Leaf prints can be made to show both the outline shape and pattern of the veins and then photographed. Begin first with simple leaves such as beech, ash, oak or sweet chestnut. The easiest way to make a leaf print is to use a wax crayon in much the same way as making a brass rubbing. The leaf (which should be as flat as possible) is placed, veins side uppermost,

Plate 15 Mature aspen *(Populus tremula)* catkins, in studio with photo-floods and artificial light colour film.

Plate 16 Male flower of goat willow *(Salix caprea)* showing individual stamens with yellow pollen. Studio, dual source oblique lighting from behind. $\times 3\frac{1}{2}$

Fig. 3.5   Multiple time lapse picture of opening sycamore (*Acer pseudoplatanus*) bud, taken at 24-hourly intervals.

beneath a sheet of good quality typing or writing paper. It is held firmly in place with one hand while the other rubs the crayon across the paper. Care should be taken not to move the paper nor to rub beyond the margins of the leaf.

Another version of this technique is to use an absorbent paper with a colourless wax pencil (or a white candle). After the print has been made, the paper is completely overwashed with a water-colour paint, so that the veins appear white against the rest of the coloured leaf. Photographs of these leaf prints have an artistic appeal and yet they still portray an accurate record of the leaf's structure. They are therefore ideal for teaching purposes through-out the year, and they are also useful as backgrounds for montage prints.

Photograms   A photographic image – made without using a camera, by the action of light on a light sensitive surface – is known as a photogram. Even if no dark-room facilities are avail-able, photograms are easily made. Any light sensitive paper, including photographic printing paper and some photocopying papers, can be used. Photocopying paper has the advantage that being slow to react, it can be used in a room darkened by drawing the curtains; whereas photographic printing paper can be handled only in a dark room with safe lights. As well as the paper, photo-graphic print developer and a fixer are required. If no photo-graphic dishes are available, use rectangular plastic washing-up bowls instead. For the light source, use either an enlarger or else a clear bulb held above the paper.

For same-size reproductions, choose either simple leaves with a striking outline or delicate sprays of leaves. Lay the paper with the light sensitive side uppermost, beneath the enlarger or the light source. Then place the leaf on top of the paper. If necessary, flatten the leaf with a sheet of glass. Switch on the light source and make sure neither the paper nor the subject is moved during the exposure.

To determine the correct exposure, with the maximum con-trast, make a test strip by exposing portions of the printing paper at regular time intervals. Develop, wash and fix the paper. Switch on the main room light to see the correct time for the richest black tones. Figure 3.6 was made on grade 2 Bromide paper by exposing for 60 seconds with the enlarger set at mini-mum aperture at 75cm from the paper. A point source of light is essential for ensuring that all parts of a 3-dimensional subject appear as a sharp silhouette. Enlarged photograms can be made

Plate 17 Red mangrove (*Rhizophora mangle*) roots photographed from a boat late in the evening, Galapagos.

Plate 18 Coco-de-mer palm (*Lodoicea maldivica*) endemic to the Seychelles, produces the largest seed in the world. Taken against the light with a long lens (opposite).

Fig. 3.6   Photogram of skeleton *Magnolia* leaf.

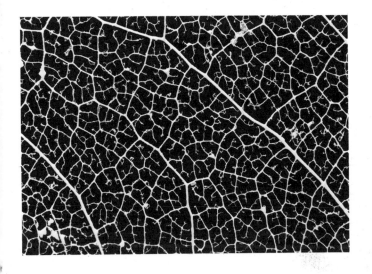

Fig. 3.7 Photogram of enlarged part of *Magnolia* skeleton leaf. × 4

of a flat translucent or perforated subject, such as a skeleton leaf, by placing it in the negative carrier of the enlarger. The magnified image is then projected and focused onto the paper in the usual way. Figure 3.7 is a photogram of an enlarged portion of the magnolia leaf shown in Fig. 3.6.

Photograms are fun. Direct prints of a negative image can be made very quickly without spending time exposing and developing a negative. Because the subject has to be removed from the paper each time a same-size photogram is made, each print is genuinely unique. A single subject – especially if it is a 3-dimensional one – can provide endless possible pictures. If a positive print is required, use a piece of sheet film in place of the printing paper to obtain a negative, and then contact print onto the paper.

Plate 19 Sycamore (*Acer pseudoplatanus*) tree in autumn, highlighted by hills in shadow behind.

Plate 20   Freshly fallen beech (*Fagus sylvatica*) and oak (*Quercus robur*) leaves
floating on water.

Fig. 4.1 Flowers of Pacific dogwood (*Cornus nuttallii*) taken with long focus lens.

Flowers of trees, apart from ornamental trees grown specifically for their flowers, often pass unnoticed. One reason is that on many trees the flowers are small compared with the tree as a whole, and also they tend to grow on the uppermost branches where they receive most sunlight. Yet when seen in close-up, the flowers of some quite common trees are exquisite.

Flowers are the sex organs of a tree: male flowers produce pollen to pollinate and fertilize the female flowers. Flowers of forest trees, such as pine, beech and oak, which are pollinated by the wind, tend to be inconspicuous in size and colour; whereas insect-pollinated flowers such as magnolias, cherries and most evergreen tropical trees, tend to be either large and showy or scented. Monoecious trees such as alder, beech, hazel, plane, sycamore and most conifers, have both male and female flowers developing on the same tree; while dioecious trees (including ginkgo, yew, juniper, holly and willow) produce either all male or all female flowers on each tree.

There is no month of the year when tree flowers cannot be found. But the majority of temperate trees flower in the spring – often before the leaves open – so that the fruit will have several months in which to ripen. It is both an increase in temperature and in the daylight hours which stimulate buds to open in the spring. Therefore the date when a particular species comes into flower depends on the latitude, and also on the altitude. Spring comes early in San Francisco (37°N); it comes late in Edinburgh (56°N). But regardless of the latitude, the order in which each species of tree comes into flower is remarkably constant. In the tropics, on the other hand, the length of daylight and darkness remains nearly always equal. There are no seasons comparable with temperate regions.

On the tree

Catkins   Tassel-like spikes of tiny flowers are known as catkins. Some of the most conspicuous are hazel, birch, alder, poplar, walnut and oak. Catkins of most deciduous trees open before or with the leaves so that the wind-blown pollen has a better chance of reaching the female flowers. Sweet chestnut is notable in producing huge cream catkins in mid-summer, when the tree is in

Plate 21   Autumnal colours beside Derwent Water, Lake District.

Plate 22   Autumnal leaves of Virginia creeper (*Parthenocissus tricuspidata*).

full leaf. When the buds open and the catkins begin to burst, some deciduous trees develop an obvious colour cast, such as the red glow at the top of black poplars.

Most catkins are fairly small and slender and so they are difficult to photograph *in situ*, unless they can be taken in close-up on a young tree or on the lower branches of older trees. None the less, useful pictures can be taken in the field, showing the overall shape and colour of these flowers. Extreme close-ups showing the detailed anatomy of individual flowers on the spike at magnifications of 2–3 times life size on the negative or the transparency, are more suitable as subjects for indoor photography.

Timing is all important for good pictures of catkins. At the stage when they shed their pollen, catkins are lax (Fig. 4.3) rather than tight. Once they have shed their pollen, and especially if they have been subjected to heavy rain, catkins are past their best. To capture the typical mobile dangling form, use either a fast shutter speed or flashlight (Fig. 4.3). Catkins on bare branches can be isolated against sky or water. Conspicuous yellow hazel catkins often show up to advantage back-lit by a shaft of sunlight against a hedgerow in shadow. Yellow flowers of conifers tend to contrast well against the dark evergreen needles.

Flowers Trees with conspicuous showy flowers such as rhododendrons, tulip tree, magnolia and eucalyptus or gum trees, are much easier to photograph in the field than the tiny male flowers of Wellingtonia, Lawson cypress or Western hemlock. A blue sky is an obvious natural background for both coloured and white flowers growing at the ends of branches. Very often a long focus lens used from ground level will be ideal for these larger flowers; but sometimes it may be better to climb up above the ground so as to look down into the flower.

Eucalyptus flowers are particularly good subjects for a photo sequence, because they are unique in having a flower bud with a lid. This falls off to reveal the numerous stamens inside. Maples are good value both in the spring when the flowers open in clusters, and in autumn when the leaves turn spectacular colours.

Flowers with large white or pastel-coloured petals such as magnolia, are more difficult to photograph successfully in bright sunlight than red flowers. The harsh lighting and strong shadows associated with direct sunlight obscures any subtle texture in the petals. Also, either the flower itself appears over-exposed or else the dark foliage appears under-exposed. For these flowers, the diffuse light which is produced on hazy or overcast days, is ideal for showing detailed texture.

Like the sweet chestnut, limes flower in mid-summer when the trees are in full leaf. Lime flowers, which are such a favourite of honeybees, tend to hang down beneath the leaves where the level of available light is low. If a wind is blowing, flashlight may be the only solution. But remember that the intensity of flashlight falls off very rapidly, so that unless the leaves and flowers fill the frame, the distant background behind the branch will appear completely black. Sometimes flashlight can be invaluable for filling in shadows on a sunny day to produce what is known as a *synchro-sunlight* shot. The appropriate shutter speed is selected by calculating the exposure for the sunlight. The flash is then moved back to where it will light the subject at the same intensity as the sunlight. This distance is determined by using the exposure calculator on the flash itself, or by calculation using the given film speed and the guide number of the flash.

Larches are deciduous conifers which produce beautiful flowers early in spring just as the new needles are bursting. These larch 'roses', as they are known, are exquisite subjects for close-up photography both outside and indoors (Plate 12).

Cones and fruit   Cones and fruit are produced after the female flower has been pollinated and fertilized. Their function is to produce seeds to disperse the species. Ginkgos and conifers are primitive seed-bearing plants belonging to the Gymnosperms. Unlike true flowering plants (the Angiosperms), the female ovules are not enclosed within an ovary; instead they form on top of seed leaves inside the female cones. These cones have to open to allow wind-blown pollen to reach the naked ovules. After pollination, the outside of the cone grows so as to enclose the ovules until they have grown and developed into ripe seeds, when the cone dries and separates to release the seeds. In the Angiosperms, the ovules develop after pollination into the seeds; while the ovary develops into the fruit.

The structure of the seed itself or of the fruit containing it, plays a vital part in its dispersal. Yew, in common with many tropical trees, produces a brightly coloured fleshy casing (the aril) to the seed, so as to attract birds or other animals. Mountain ash, hawthorn and cherries likewise develop highly coloured skins to their fruit. Oak acorns and beech mast are also dispersed by birds and mammals which often horde them during the

Plate 23   Knee roots of swamp cypress *(Taxodium distichum)* growing up
along water's edge (opposite).

Plate 24   Sun setting behind dead mangroves in the Galapagos Islands.

winter. Fruits which split to expose their seeds are known as dehiscent. This type of mechanical dispersal can be seen in the pods which are produced by members of the pea family, including the false acacias and the laburnums (Fig. 4.2).

Many of the temperate trees which flower in early spring, produce seeds which are wind-dispersed either by small hairy parachutes (poplars and willows), or by winged seeds (elms). Conifers and maples also produce winged seeds. On hot sunny days, pine cones distinctly crack, as they dry and split open to release their winged seeds.

One important point to remember before searching for cones and fruit to photograph, is that they can develop only from female flowers. Therefore, while they are always likely to be present on trees which produce both male and female flowers on the same tree, they will never occur on the male trees of dioecious species.

The position of the flowers and hence the fruit on the tree, is to some extent determined by the size and weight of the fruit. Flowers which produce lightweight cones or fruit tend to develop on or near the tips of the youngest shoots. Although trees such as pine, may bear their female flowers at the tip of a new young shoot, and by the time the cones mature over two years later, they are supported by a woody branch. Whereas flowers of tropical trees which produce large, heavy fruit such as the cannon-ball tree, the durian and the jak fruit tree are borne directly on the trunk.

Palms produce their nuts on inflorescences, quite distinct from the leaves, at the top of the trunk. The easiest way to photograph these palm fruits is to stand at the base of the tree and look straight up the bole. Leaves, or even parts of leaves, included in a picture of fruit can add both colour and interest. Sunlight streaming through the leaf bases of the coco-de-mer palm in Plate 18 has helped to relieve the solid nature of the huge fruit.

The large upright owl-like cones produced by cedars and firs (*Abies* spp.) stand out more clearly against the foliage than drooping Douglas fir, spruce or pine cones. Cedar and fir cones should be photographed as soon as they have turned brown, as unlike pine and spruce cones, they break up while still attached to the tree, leaving only the central peg. As the best specimens of fruit and cones are so often high up a tree, a long focus lens will be invaluable for photographing larger specimens. Alternatively, climb up a step-ladder or bring the branch down to a lower level by tying it down with wire or elasticated luggage straps. Planes

Fig. 4.2   Laburnum (*Laburnum anagyroides*) dehiscing. Available evening light.

and jacaranda are both deciduous trees on which the fruit persists after leaf-fall. The characteristic plane bobbles and the large circular jacaranda pods make striking winter silhouettes.

There are also the unexpected pictures which arise without any planning or forethought. When I saw the cluster of raffia fruit for sale in the Seychelles, their rich golden colour, combined with their shiny surface, suggested the impact close-up picture shown in Plate 11. So here is an instance of fruit being photographed out of doors – but remote from its tree. This technique is perfectly acceptable if it is used to illustrate detailed structure and colour; in fact it may well help to clarify the shape by permitting better lighting or a less confusing background to be selected. The dehiscing laburnum pods were not photographed *in situ* on the tree. They were collected and photographed in my garden using the low angled light of the late afternoon sun. This helped to accentuate the dark seeds inside the pale pod (Fig. 4.2).

Seed dispersal is generally a difficult subject to illustrate well in the field. With patience, the white fluffy seeds of poplars and willows can be photographed being blown away from their catkin; but the keys of maples and sycamore spiral down to the ground almost faster than it is possible to focus the camera. These seeds as well as elm seeds and the larger horse and sweet chestnut fruit, can be photographed when they have fallen to the ground by using a ground spike with a ball and socket head to support the camera.

Portraits

Flowers and fruit   Very often more detail, and hence more information, will be gained from critical close-up portraits of catkins, flowers, fruit and cones taken indoors. As already mentioned for leaves, careful selection of both light sources and background colour can highlight some particular feature of the subject. Plate 14 shows more than a sharply focused close-up of a few horse chestnut flowers; it shows how the colour of the centre of the flower changes with age. Compare this with the typical picture of a complete flower spike on the tree; which at most will show a collection of white flowers with pink centres.

If flowers are picked with little or no stem, they will soon wilt inside a heated room. The heat generated by photoflood lamps will accelerate this wilting. Therefore, either pick the flower with enough stalk for it to be contained in a vessel of water, or else photograph it as quickly as possible – preferably with a light source which emits little or no heat.

Fig. 4.3 Silver birch (*Betula pendula*) catkins dispersing pollen. Studio, dual source oblique lighting with electronic flash from behind. ×2

Fig. 4.4 Enlarged portion of Wellingtonia (*Sequoiadendron giganteum*) cone. Single grazed light source. × 6½

Small flowers and cones look more natural and are easier to manœuvre for photography, if they are kept attached to their foliage as in Plate 8. Larger flowers, fruit or cones which have a well-defined outline can be photographed in isolation. If the subject is laid directly onto black velvet, there will be no shadow problem; but if a pale coloured background is selected the direction of the lighting is much more critical. One simple technique is to rest the subject on the lower portion of a flexible board, which curves up behind the subject. By using either indirect bounced lighting or by using a direct light source overhead and slightly in front of the subject, no obvious shadows will be seen. Alternatively, the shadows cast by oblique lighting of the subject can be directed outside the field of view by raising the subject up from the background on a sheet of plate glass. Mount the camera on a copying stand or a copipod vertically above the sheet of glass. Focus the camera on the subject and if shadows appear in the field of view, move the light sources further away from the subject and reduce their angle to the glass. The cluster of magnolia fruit in Plate 13 was supported on a piece of glass and photographed in this way. Individual winged seeds of conifers, elm or maple can also be photographed raised up from the background, by transmitted light of a light box (page 52) or by dark field illumination (page 52).

Catkins and cones   Both catkins and cones are excellent subjects for photographing indoors at successively greater magnifications. By working indoors, much more dramatic lighting can be used to emphasize their 3-dimensional structure. Dual source oblique lighting from behind was used both in Plate 16 to capture the multitude of individual stamens in a single pussy willow catkin and to spotlight the pollen cloud in Fig. 4.3.

Pictures showing comparative shape and size of cones, are best taken indoors against a unicoloured or toned background. Portions of large cones make exciting patterns or designs. Figure 4.4 shows part of a Wellingtonia cone lit by a single grazed light source so that each scale is sharply outlined against a shadow area. Critical focusing for studio close-ups will be made easier by mounting the camera onto a focusing slide instead of directly onto a tripod.

Fig. 5.1 Beech (*Fagus sylvatica*) fruit and leaves

CHAPTER 5   AUTUMNAL COLOURS

Without doubt more colour film is exposed on the autumn (the fall) colours of deciduous trees than on any other trees or parts of trees at any other time of year. The European beeches, the North American maples, sweet gums and scarlet oaks bring brilliant splashes of colour to an otherwise rather drab landscape. Autumn is always a pleasant time in which to visit the English Lake District, but I remember 1973 as being a particularly spectacular year. Early in the morning, splashes of colour began to loom out from the valley mists. Then as the sun filtered through the mists a riot of colour appeared as the birches, beeches, sycamores and larches turned and retained their own distinctive autumn shades for days on end, in beautiful calm conditions.

Production of colour

Each species turns its own characteristic colour – which may be consistently good – or it may vary from one year to another. The best autumn tints develop after a warm summer followed by low temperatures, which need not be below freezing; indeed frosts may damage the leaves.

How do these colours arise? As the daylight hours decrease and the amount of darkness lengthens each day, the rate of photosynthesis in the leaves slows down, as the production of the green pigment known as chlorophyll also slows down and finally ceases. As the amount of chlorophyll within a leaf is reduced, then other pigments, which were previously masked by the green, become visible. Yellow carotenoid pigments are commonly present in many autumn leaves, while the red colouring of some maples and American oaks is due to anthocyanin pigments which mask the yellow colours. Because the development of these water soluble red pigments relates directly to the weather, their extent varies from year to year.

Light stimulates the production of anthocyanins, so that the most exposed leaves will also be the most highly coloured; whereas leaves in shadow are slow to turn and may never develop a rich colour. If there is an extended period of drought at the end of the summer, the leaves will tend to shrivel and turn brown on the trees rather than develop autumnal colours. Eventually deciduous leaves are shed so that the tree will not lose precious water when the ground is frozen, by evaporation through the leaf surface.

To do justice to the array of colours which appear in autumnal leaves, most of the photographs relating to this chapter are reproduced here in colour. For a colour photograph to have impact, it does not have to be a blatant splash of red. It can be a subtle range of yellows, golds and browns clustering in a valley (Plate 21), or a translucent pinky brown of sunlight streaming through black gum leaves (Plate 7).

Landscapes

While autumn colour in some form can be seen over a period of several weeks, the peak may last for a few days only. Therefore there is always the tendency to rush around photographing as quickly as possible without much care and thought in varying the approach. The techniques for photographing groups of trees or isolated trees will follow the same guide lines given in Chapter 1, but the emphasis here will be on colour, rather than on shape and form.

Both in an open woodland or on a hillside, a shaft of sunlight may selectively highlight one tree or a group of trees amongst the surrounding neighbouring trees in deep shadow. The red light cast by a low angled sun can be used to emphasize autumnal colours. A haze filter which is used for penetrating haze, may eliminate the autumnal atmosphere altogether. Such an atmosphere can be increased so that it resembles the landscapes of French impressionists, by using a special soft focus lens or a diffusing lens attached to the front of a normal lens, combined with a slow shutter speed. A polarizing filter can produce particularly dramatic autumnal scenes.

Once leaf fall has begun, more light will penetrate through the overhead canopy to reach the floor below. This makes woodland photography without a tripod, somewhat easier. For a short time it will be possible to photograph trees which have retained some leaves – and therefore some colour – as well as showing the shape of the trunk and the branching pattern. If this critical stage can be captured, it can provide as much information as a bare winter skeleton – with the added interest of colour.

For a convincing photograph of leaves falling, several calm days, followed by a day of intermittent breezy gusts, is ideal. Once again, a shaft of sunlight will highlight the leaves better than an overall blanket of sun. For clear images of individual leaves in mid-air, use as fast a shutter speed as possible. Whereas a slow shutter speed will result in blurred leaf images which may convey better the downward movement.

Close-ups

Brightly coloured branches with a few leaves, can be isolated equally well against a clear blue or a dull grey sky. *Contre jour* or against the light pictures of leaves almost seem to glow, as the sunlight streams through them (Plate 7). For even greater impact, look for a chance to use this type of lighting when the background is in deep shadow. Part of a trunk or a bough silhouetted in the foreground will complement the bright colours of a mosaic of transilluminated leaves behind.

While some of the most spectacular colours are produced by deciduous broadleaved trees, the deciduous conifers should not be forgotten. Some produce very subtle colours: the swamp cypress turns a pinky brown before ending up a deep foxy red. The dawn redwood turns creamy gold and finally becomes a pinkish amber colour. Also the warm gold produced by larches in autumn is well worth recording.

Even when leaves have fallen from the tree, they can still make photographs. Freshly fallen leaves will float on water, and both the shape and colour show up well on the water surface (Plate 20). On the forest floor, leaves form carpets of colour. Look also for green moss cushions as a contrast to the brown leaves. By shedding their leaves each autumn, deciduous trees begin each spring with a complete new set of intact, uneaten leaves. Recently fallen autumn leaves which are still flat, are good subjects for indoor photography by transmitted light, using a light box (page 52). The variation in leaf shape and colour on a single tree or between different trees can be compared. It is certainly preferable to collect autumn leaves from the ground than to pick living leaves from a tree. Also, they will not shrivel up so quickly as fresh young leaves.

Fig. 6.1   Aerial roots of black mangrove
(*Avicennia marina*). Seychelles.

Roots are the hidden part of most trees and so they are photo-graphed much less frequently than the trunk or the leaves. Yet to a tree, roots are just as vital. They anchor the tree to the ground, they absorb water and minerals in solution from the soil and transport them to the aerial part of the tree. Roots also store food. When roots become exposed, it is only the largest ones which we see. The important absorbing part of the root system is made up of minute root tips and hairs.

All roots begin as vertical tap roots. Trees such as the oak, which continue to develop the tap root as well as some side anchoring roots, are much more likely to withstand high winds than shallow rooting birches and beeches. These trees develop many horizontal roots close to the surface and so are prone to wind-felling. The extent of the root system depends much more on the nature of the soil than on the type of tree. It is well known that some trees grow better on one type of soil than another. Under favourable conditions for growth, a root system may branch out into a much wider circumference than the crown of the tree. Conversely, repeated pruning of the root system pre-vents upward growth of the trunk and branches and results in the abnormal miniature bonsai trees.

Exposed roots

Roots which normally develop below ground level, can become exposed by erosion of a bank or a hillside, by gales tearing up a shallow-rooted tree or by rough seas undermining a cliff face. Erosion of roots on a bank can be a very gradual process, taking many years before enough roots have become exposed to warrant taking a photograph. If the bank rises steeply from the road, track or stream, both the lighting and the viewpoint will be limited. Lighting angled along the length of the bank will repeat the root shapes in a shadow pattern. If a site is already known, check the orientation of the bank on a map to determine the time of day when the lighting will be most suitable. The viewpoint will be determined both by the lighting, and by the accessibility of the bank.

It is worth going out after a storm in search of wind-felled trees – especially for shallow-rooting beech, birch, spruces and poplars. In heathland areas podsols occur which are underlain by a hard iron pan. Trees in general in these areas will therefore be shallow-rooting and will be more susceptible to being felled by high winds.

A photograph taken end-on to the root mass will be dramatic, but will not convey the length of the trunk which the roots supported – unless it is resting on sloping ground. On flat ground the root ball and the trunk will be visible only from the side.

Aerial roots

Not all roots are subterranean. In tropical countries, several types of trees develop prop roots which grow down from a branch or the side of the tree to provide additional support.

Mangroves, which are a common feature of tropical estuaries, produce copious aerial roots. The red mangrove, which can grow up to 30 metres high, sends out horizontal roots which branch before finally gaining a foothold amongst the sand or rocks. Eventually, a dense intertwining thicket forms, which traps sediments and leaves. A well-established red mangrove swamp is therefore difficult to penetrate on foot and often can be photographed only from the outside on the shore or in a boat (Plate 17). The best time for photographing mangrove roots is at low water, when they are completely exposed and there is less depth of water to wade through on foot. On colour film, both the green leaves and the red roots of the red mangrove will contrast well against rocks or the sea. Whereas in monochrome, a silhouette of one or a few trees will emphasize better the shape of the tree and the extent of the whole root system.

It is possible to walk amongst the interior of some mangrove swamps, but the lighting is so poor that a tripod is essential. The legs will have to be immersed in brackish water, so preferably use a wooden tripod or else remember to thoroughly wash and dry a metallic one after use. To give some idea of the poor light conditions, when using a film speed of 25 ASA, with an aperture of f/5.6, the exposure was $\frac{1}{2}$ a second inside a Galapagos button mangrove swamp.

Black mangroves have horizontal roots which creep beneath the mud and send up short vertical aerial roots. In amongst these roots is a favourite haunt of fiddler crabs. Lighting the short aerial roots is clearly no problem, but walking amongst them is certainly uncomfortable. For monochrome pictures, harsh uni-directional lighting as in Fig. 6.1 is usually the most effective. When working with colour filmstock, look for an additional splash of colour, such as a young sapling with green leaves growing up amongst the roots.

84

Fig. 6.2 Beech (*Fagus sylvatica*) roots exposed by eroding bank.

The swamp or bald cypress which is native to the south-east United States and Mexico, as its name suggests favours swampy moist places. In the Florida Everglades the trees are festooned with curtains of Spanish moss. The swamp cypress, which is a deciduous conifer, is extensively planted outside the United States. Its most striking features are the conical 'knees' – a metre or more high – which project from the water like small termite mounds (Plate 23). These stumpy projections, or breathing roots, are thought to supply oxygen to the water-logged roots.

The screwpines are a group of palm-like shrubs or trees which produce extensive stilt-like roots. These plants, which have spirally-arranged leaves (Fig. 3.1), form a conspicuous part of the flora in several Indian Ocean islands. In the Seychelles, where the screwpines are known as vacoas, one endemic species called vacoa marron, grows up to 14 metres high amongst rocky outcrops. It sends out prop roots – up to 30 metres long – into ravines below. Very often the original trunk rots away so that the prop roots become the sole means of support. Such trees sway eerily in the wind. In the mountain mist forest on Mahé, the older aerial roots become clothed with epiphytic mosses. The accessible vacoas can be photographed only by shooting up towards the sky.

One of the most spectacular growths of aerial roots is produced by the banyan tree. This tree, which is sacred to the Hindus, belongs to the fig family. A seed, dropped at random on a host tree by a bird, germinates to form a plant which grows initially as an epiphyte, sending down aerial roots to the ground. These roots then thicken, become trunk-like and send out more side branches. Finally, the banyan ends up as a complex system of vertical, diagonal and horizontal struts covering an extensive area – one tree provided sufficient shelter for 20,000 people.

Fig. 6.3   Prop roots of latanier latte palm (*Verschaffeltia splendida*). Seychelles (opposite).

CHAPTER 7   DECAYING TREES

Even trees which have died and maybe lost their finer branches
and bark, provide an endless source of photographic subjects.
Death may result from natural causes or from the activity of the
tree feller.

Standing trees

Dead standing trees may have been killed by lightning strike,
fungal attack, flooding or even by being ring-barked by mammals. Death is followed by the shedding of twigs and bark,
gradual decay and the invasion of many insects, hole-nesting
birds and even roosting bats.

Silhouetted against darkening clouds, a gaunt tree skeleton can
give an eerie atmosphere to a photograph. Whether positioned
in the foreground of the frame or as background interest, a dead
tree can be used to provide a startling contrast between life and
death. Nature is a constant cycle of birth and decay.

Lake Naivasha in Kenya covered with water-lilies and fringed
with papyrus reeds, is a beautiful lake because of, rather than in
spite of, dozens of dead bleached trees projecting from the water.
These trees, which were killed by a sudden rise in the water level,
add another dimension to the lake. Darters, pelicans, egrets and
fish eagles all use these trees as perching places.

Fallen trees

Old trees, especially those weakened by heart wood fungal
attack, are often brought crashing down in gales. Once a tree has
fallen it becomes a most complex microhabitat. Insects and other
animals colonize it to feed on the wood, the attacking fungus or
even other invaders. The trunk may shelter a fox's lair, and the
stump provide an owl with a perch or squirrels with a feeding
site. Other plants colonize the trunk and rotting wood. Lichens,
mosses and ferns occur in profusion.

These crumbling old trees, which are the breeding sites of
several rare insects, tend to be torn to pieces by over-zealous

---

Fig. 7.1   TL   Callus in old holly (*Ilex aquifolium*).
       BL   Face in old oak trunk (*Quercus robur*).
       TR   White fork moss (*Leucobryum glaucum*) growing in cracks of fallen
           oak trunk.
       BR   Felled larches (*Larix decidua*) end-on.

entomologists hunting larvae and pupae. Tidy-minded woods-men cut them and burn them. Perhaps now that we are all be-coming much more conservation conscious, more of these dead giants will be allowed to rot slowly away. The gradual disinte-gration of a fallen tree could provide the subject of a most ex-citing long term photographic essay for the nature photographer, taxing all aspects of his skill and knowledge.

Felled trees Even the activities of a forester's saw can be a source of tree pictures. The circular annual rings show up most clearly on recently felled trees (Fig. 7.1 BR). Each of these rings which are distinctive in temperate trees, represents the amount of new wood which is added each year. In the spring, the wood has large vessels; whereas later in the summer the vessels are smaller and this 'late wood' is distinctively coloured.

The growth rings can be used not only to age temperate trees but also to assess past changes in climate. The better the climate, the more growth occurs and so the rings appear more widely spaced apart. During unfavourable seasons, including periods of drought, narrow rings are formed. Even live standing trees can be aged by taking core samples of the wood. This is the way the Californian bristlecone pines were aged and found to be the oldest living things on Earth – some are over 4000 years old.

In the tropics where there is no clear seasonal cycle, many trees do not have rings. If rings are present in tropical trees, they may represent the flowering or fruiting cycle which may not be annual.

Wood sections Photographs of wood sections are best taken either of recently felled trees or of varnished or polished sections. Polishing prevents cracking of the heart wood, but presents the same problem to the photographer as with any shiny object. With small sections, use indirect diffuse lighting to reduce re-flections of the light source. With large sections, reflections from shiny parts of the camera and tripod will be an additional prob-lem, unless all but the centre of the lens is masked off with a matt black board.

Shapes in wood

On land; rain, wind, frost, ice and sun and despoilation by ani-mals all contribute into eroding away wood and moulding it into distorted or beautiful shapes. The sea, with its pounding waves and grinding sand is even more effective at sculpturing wood into fantastic shapes – shapes which can vary from abstract art form to close resemblances to natural objects – including human faces.

Only by critical appraisal of the direction and type of lighting can the texture of wood be shown to full advantage. Both pictures in Fig. 7.2 were taken by indirect low intensity available light as the sun was setting late in the evening.

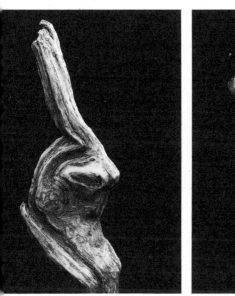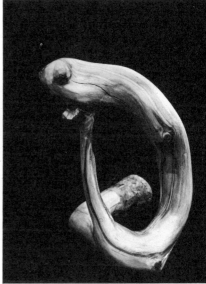

Fig. 7.2   Two natural sculptures in wood.

APPENDICES
A PHOTOGRAPHIC GLOSSARY

Aperture   Iris diaphragm of lens which controls amount of light reaching film. Calibrated in 'numerical apertures' (f numbers or stops) which change by a factor of 1.4 ($\sqrt{2}$) in one stop increments in series 1, 1.4, 2, 2.8, 4, ... 16, 22 . . . .

Artificial light film   Colour filmstock for use with photofloods or household light bulbs.

Ball-and-socket head   Attached to tripod or other support to allow tilt and rotation of camera or flash.

Bellows   Variable extension inserted between the lens and the camera body for close-up photography, allowing magnifications of greater than life size (1:1).

Bounced lighting   Indirect diffuse lighting obtained by shining the light source(s) onto a white board, wall or umbrella, above or to one side of the subject.

Close-up lens (Supplementary lens)   Fitted to front of camera lens for close-up photography.

Colour cast   Unnatural colouring either due to using the incorrect film with a particular lighting (e.g. daylight film with photofloods) or to reflection from a coloured surface.

Contrast filters   Strongly coloured filters used with monochrome films to lighten or darken a subject so as to isolate it from its surroundings.

Conversion filter   Used with colour films to correct overall colour balance for a film designed to be used at a different colour temperature, e.g. blue Wratten 80B used with daylight colour films and photoflood lighting; and orange Wratten 85 used with artificial light colour films in daylight.

Copipod   Camera support with four legs used for overhead photography, especially copying work.

Dark field illumination   Transmitted lighting, in which the subject appears brightly lit against a black background. Suitable for hairy and translucent subjects.

Depth of field   Zone of sharp focus behind and in front of plane of focus. Increased by using a smaller aperture or by decreasing the image size. Particularly important in close-up work, when the depth of field becomes reduced.

Diaphragm shutter   Iris-type shutter usually positioned between the lens elements, but sometimes behind or in front. Synchronized with electronic flash at all speeds.

Diffuse lighting   Soft lighting which produces soft edged shadows, and least obvious highlights on shiny objects.

Electronic flash   Reusable flash which produces an instantaneous discharge in a gas-filled tube.

Exposure   Correct combination of shutter speed and lens aperture to produce a satisfactory negative or transparency for a given film speed and a particular light intensity.

Extension tubes   Inserted between the camera body and the lens for close-up photography. Automatic tubes allow retention of fully automatic diaphragm mechanism.

Film speed   Relative sensitivity of a film to light, expressed either as an ASA or a DIN rating. 'Slow' films have a low rating and require more light than 'fast' films.

Filter   Alters the nature of light passing through the lens to the film, by absorbing particular wavelengths.

Flare   Bright spots or patches formed by strong light reflections inside the lens, when the camera is pointed towards a light source. Flare can be reduced by using a lens hood or a multi-coated lens.

Focal plane shutter   Camera shutter positioned immediately in front of the film plane, made of fabric or metal blinds.

Focus   Adjusting the lens – film distance so that the subject image appears sharp on the film plane.

Focusing slide   Used mounted on a tripod, it allows the camera to be moved towards or away from the subject for critical focusing in close-up work, without altering the magnification.

Frame   A single exposure amongst a series on a film.

Grazed lighting   (Textured lighting)   Extreme low angled oblique lighting used for emphasizing texture.

Ground spike   Camera support for ground level subjects, the base of which is pushed into the ground.

Guide number   (Flash factor)   When divided by the subject distance, indicates correct aperture (or vice versa). Does *not* apply for close-ups.

Haze filter   Absorbs unwanted ultra-violet radiation. It is especially useful when working at altitude or near large expanses of water.

Incident light reading   Measures the light falling on the subject. The light meter, with a diffuser attached, is pointed in the subject to camera direction.

Infra-red light   Long wavelengths outside the visible spectrum which penetrate haze. Special infra-red films (both monochrome and colour) are used for infra-red photography.

Lens coating   Microscopic layer covering outer lens surface which reduces flare, especially on multi-coated lenses.

Lens hood   Projects in front of lens. It reduces the possibility of back lighting striking the front surface of the lens and thereby causing flare.

Long focus lens   Has a focal length greater than the standard lens, and increases the camera to subject distance for a given image size. Covers an angle of view of less than 45°.

Macro lens   A lens with built-in extension allowing magnifications of up to at least 0·5 without using extension tubes or bellows.

Over-exposure   Due to excessive light reaching the film, colour transparencies appear thin and negatives dense.

Perspective correcting lens   Special wide angle lens used for correcting converging verticals, by means of off-centring the lens.

Photoflood   Artificial light used for studio work for monochrome and artificial light colour films.

Polarizing filter   Used to reduce distracting reflections from water and glass or wet and shiny surfaces. It also darkens a blue sky.

Reflected light reading   Measures the light reflected from the subject. The light meter is directed away from the camera towards the subject.

Reflex camera   Has ground glass screen for critical composition and focusing. Twin lens reflex (TLR) cameras have two lenses, one for viewing and one for taking, while single lens reflex (SLR) cameras have one lens only.

Ring flash   Electronic flash which encircles the camera lens. Provides frontal lighting in extreme close-ups

SLR   *See* Reflex camera.

Standard lens   Has a focal length approximately equal to the diagonal of the negative or transparency, giving an angle of view of 45-50°.

Stop   (f number)   Numerical aperture of lens iris diaphragm which controls the intensity of light reaching the film.

Synchro-sunlight   Balanced combination of sunlight and flashlight.

TTL   (Through the lens) meter   Reflected light meter built into a SLR camera which measures the light passing through the lens.

Transmitted light   Light which passes through the subject.

Under-exposure   Due to insufficient light reaching the film, colour transparencies appear dense and negatives thin.

Wide angle lens   Short focal length lens giving a wide angle of view (greater than 50°) than a standard lens used from the same position.

APPENDICES

B EQUIPMENT CHECK LIST FOR TREE PHOTOGRAPHY

Basic field equipment

Camera with standard lens $\left\{\begin{array}{l}\text{(50mm for 35mm format)}\\ \text{(80mm for 6} \times \text{6cm format)}\end{array}\right\}$ with lens hood
Light meter (if camera does not have TTL metering)
Spare batteries for TTL meter

Films	Spirit-level
Tripod	Wire for tying back branches
Cable release	Reflector
Haze filter	Secateurs
Close-up lenses	Umbrella
Lens tissues	Notebook or pocket tape-recorder
Gadget bag or rucksack	

Additional field equipment

Medium long focus lens $\left\{\begin{array}{l}\text{(105 or 135mm for 35mm format)}\\ \text{(150 or 250mm for 6} \times \text{6cm format)}\end{array}\right\}$ with lens hood
Wide angle lens $\left\{\begin{array}{l}\text{(35mm for 35mm format)}\\ \text{(50mm for 6} \times \text{6cm format)}\end{array}\right\}$ with lens hood

Contrast filters	Flash (bulb or electronic)
Polarizing filter	Copipod
Extension tubes	Table-top tripod or ground spike, with
Bellows	ball-and-socket head
Waist level or right angle viewfinder	Step-ladder
	Perspective correcting lens

Additional studio equipment

Plasticine	Photofloods
Sand	White card
Black velvet	Sheets of glass
Board backgrounds	Light box
Spotlights	

C THE NATURE PHOTOGRAPHERS' CODE OF PRACTICE

All photographers working in Britain should read the leaflet: *The Nature Photographers' Code of Practice*, produced by the Association of Natural History Photographic Societies. Copies can be obtained from the RSPB, The Lodge, Sandy, Bedfordshire, SG19 2DL, by sending a stamped addressed envelope.

D BOOKS FOR FURTHER READING AND IDENTIFICATION

* Extensively illustrated with photographs. ·
† For identification of trees.

* Angel, Heather, *Nature Photography: Its art and techniques*, Fountain Press/ M.A.P., Kings Langley, 1972.
*† Beadle, N. C. W., Evans, O. D. & Carolin, R. C., *Flora of the Sydney region*, Reed, Sydney, rev. edn. 1972.
*† Bean, W. J., *Trees and shrubs hardy in the British Isles*, 3 vols., Murray, London, Vol. 1 (8th edn.) 1970; Vol. 2 (8th edn.) 1973; Vol. 3 (7th edn.) 1951.
* Brokman, C. F., *Trees of North America*, Golden Press, N.Y., 1968.
* Corner, E. J. H., *Wayside trees of Malaya*, 2 vols., 2nd edn., Govt. Printers, Singapore, 1952.
* Dale, I. R. & Greenway, P. J., *Kenya Trees and Shrubs*, 1961.
* Everett, T. H., *Living trees of the world*, Thames and Hudson, London, 1969.
* Feininger, A., *Trees*, Thames and Hudson, London, 1968.
* Fovel, O., *Hidden art in Nature: synchromies*, Patrick Stephens, London, 1972.
*† Holliday, I., & Hill, R., *A field guide to Australian trees*, Rigby, Kent Town, 1969.
*† Hough, R. B., *Handbook of the trees of the Northern States and Canada*, Macmillan, New York, 1947.
*† Johnson, Hugh, *The international book of trees*, Mitchell Beazley, London, 1973.
*† McCurrach, J. C., *Palms of the world*, Harper Bros., New York, 1960.
*† Millet, M., *Native trees of Australia*, Lansdowne Press, Melbourne, 1971.
† Mitchell, A. F., *A field guide to the trees of Britain and Northern Europe*, Collins, London, 1974.
*† Palmer, E. & Pitman, N., *Trees of Southern Africa*, 3 vols. A. A. Balkema, Cape Town, Vol. 1 1972; Vols. 2 & 3 1973.
† Poole, A. L. & Adams, N. M., *Trees and shrubs of New Zealand*, Wellington, N.Z., 1963.
* Stainton, J. D. A., *Forests of Nepal*, John Murray, London, 1972.
*† Van Wyk, P., *Trees of the Kruger National Park*, Purnell, Cape Town, 1972.
† Whitmore, J. C. (ed.), *Tree flora of Malaya*, 2 vols. Longmans, London, Vol. 1 1972; Vol. 2 1973.
*† Worrell, E. & Sourry, L., *Trees of the Australian Bush*, Angus & Robertson, Sydney, 1968.

INDEX

Numbers in **bold** type refer to illustrations

Printed in Great Britain by W. S. Cowell Ltd, Ipswich